THE GIFT

Amanda J. Seymour, Th.M.

DEDICATION

This book is dedicated to those who have shown me the beauty of The Gift, especially my parents and my precious girls.

CONTENTS

ENDORSEMENTS

"In Amanda J. Seymour's book, *The Gift*, she expertly investigates the meaning of love as described in the Scriptures and provides ample directions for giving and receiving the most powerful gift in the world. I recommend you take the lessons contained in this book seriously and commit yourself to developing the same traits in your own life. It is the most important endeavor you will ever undertake."

Joan Hunter, Author/Evangelist
Founder and President of Joan Hunter Ministries

There is no greater gift

And no greater joy

Than loving

and being loved.

Yet many people have not come to know this joy in its entirety.

Why?

Because they have not learned what love is in *its entirety*.

This book is about how to live and give the complete gift of love to ourselves and others, the gift of true love.

INTRODUCTION

Have you ever wanted to give or receive the best gift of all? Now you can. You can give this book to someone else or give it to yourself as one of the most important gifts you could ever give or receive: the gift of love.

We have heard it said, "What the world needs now is love, sweet love." It isn't just a song. It's the truth. For many, love has become a cliché, passé, or something you just say. But it does not have to be, nor should it.

Love is the greatest gift in the world. And it is time that we got back to this wonderful truth that love is the greatest gift – and it is meant to make a life-changing difference in our lives and the lives of others.

Everyone wants to love and be loved. But do we even know what love really is?

This is one of the most important questions we could ask in our lifetimes. And many people ask it. But they just keep asking it because few people have confidence in the answer they give.

This book is intended to give you The Gift - the gift of Love - and confidence in The Gift so you can give The Gift to others with certainty!

That is what this book is about.

Why I Wrote This Book

One day, I told a friend that I was writing a book about love. "I am calling it *The Gift,*" I told her. "*The Gift?* Why would you do that?" she said. "There are all kinds of books on love. Who would read it?"

I knew what she was implying. Lots of books have already been written on love. Why would anyone even think to read a book about it? Well, even if you have read many books on love, you have not read this one. And this book contains the most comprehensive teaching about what love really is and how to know when love is true love.

As my friend and I discussed the book further, she said "Everyone knows what love is." But I kindly disagree.

Most people know what love in general but can they describe it specifically? Can you? We all know we want to love and be loved. But what is love, really? And how do we love well? These are the deeper questions about love which must be answered.

Wouldn't you like to know the answers to these questions? I believe the question of love is one of the most important questions anyone could ever ask. I wanted to find the answers and be able to help others as well in their quest to better understand true love. So I conducted research and wrote this book.

Gaining a deeper understanding about love helps us achieve greater fulfillment and triumph in our lives. If we look closely at the times in our lives when we are facing heartache, heartbreak, or challenging times in relationships – whether with a romantic partner, friendship, family, or our faith, the question of what we understand love to be and how to love will make all the difference in our ability to get through those times in victory rather than defeat.

I was raised in a loving family. But for many years, I did not have a mature understanding of love. I have been through both good and challenging times in my life. In my 20s, I experienced an abusive marriage, miscarriage, the death of a parent, divorce, and single motherhood. My understanding of love carried and strengthened me through these hard times. It also gave me the strength I needed to take my life to the next level in the future. I now have a fulfilling life full of love, joy, hope, and promise.

I wrote this book because I truly believe love is the greatest gift we could ever give or receive but it is the least understood. We assume we know what love is but after heartbreaks and heartaches we find ourselves asking, "How do I know when love is true?" I have found that to be the case in my own life, anyway. And I am not just talking about in romantic relationships, but in all kinds of relationships, really, including romantic relationships, family relationships, friendships, and acquaintances. We often experience the deepest love wounds in romantic relationships, but we experience hurt, disappointment, and disregard in other relationships, too. These love wounds make us squeamish to give ourselves freely to others in love.

In my own life, I have always sought a deeper and fuller understanding of love – toward God, myself, and others. Heartbreak and loss have also caused me to ask, "What is love, really?" and "Was that love?"

The more I have come to understand about love, this understanding has helped me become better at discerning true love, loving others well, and learning to fill my life and relationships with love.

We must not let ourselves grow stale in our assumptions about love because love is not meant to be commonplace or cliché! It is the most amazing gift we have ever been given. It is meant to awaken and enliven us to live our lives to the greatest meaning, purpose, and gift that one could ever have or give!

What we need is more confidence about how to recognize true love, how to love truly, and how to discern when something is not love-based. If we knew the difference, we could walk in confidence and be more secure and loving in our own right. And we could also be wiser and more discerning in sharing our hearts with others who know how to love and protecting our hearts from those who don't.

It is my hope that this book on *The Gift* of love will awaken us to the wonder of love and help us grow in our understanding and ability to give and receive it in our lives and the lives of others.

Who This Book Is For

This book is for anyone and everyone seeking the best gift they could ever give or receive: the gift of love. I wrote this book for myself and for you, dear reader. I wanted to know what love really is. And I wanted to share the wonderful truths I discovered about love with you.

This book is for anyone who wants to understand love more fully. It is for people who want to know, "Am I loveable?" or, "How do I love others well?" It is especially written with victims of broken relationships, abuse, and human trafficking in mind, and anyone else who wants to grow in their ability to love and be loved more wisely, fully, and deeply.

It is my hope that as we learn what love is, it would enrich our lives and the lives of those to whom we give The Gift.

PART I. THE GIFT

The Gift I want to give you is the gift of love. It is a love that is deeper, wider and more comprehensive than anything you may be going through. When you receive it, it will cover you like a blanket, giving you greater security, protection and peace. It will add comfort, awe and wonder to your life. And it will steady your heart and mind, adding deeper confidence and security to your thoughts, emotions and spirit.

The Gift of Love

In our lifetime, we will give and receive many gifts. These include tangible gifts, like birthday and holiday presents, money, clothing, food, and special mementos. Life itself is a gift. Time is a gift. Our homes, schooling, and relationships are gifts. Yet the greatest gift of all is love. If you have love, you have everything. If you don't have love, no matter what you have, it ultimately feels empty and void. Love is the most important gift we could ever give or receive.

There is no replacement for and nothing greater than love. If we have love, we have everything. If we do not have it, no matter what else we have, it will never be enough, for us or for others.

Yet we must learn how to recognize love and to make loving the highest priority in our lives.

Recognizing Love

Many people will come into our lives in the name of love. But how do we know when their love is true? Whether they are a romantic interest, family, friend, or acquaintance, there are several qualities which love effervesces when it is real love. We must learn to recognize these qualities. We will discuss the attributes of love shortly.

Think of the people you know whom you consider to be your truest friends and family. You consider them closest to you because you *know* they love and care for you and have your best interest at heart.

You may not always like to hear what they have to say. But you *know* they are always *for* you and want to see you live into your *best*. No matter how much time has passed, it feels like just yesterday since you spoke, saw each other or spent time together. These qualities are the signature of love.

On the other hand, if a person says they love you but they are acting in ways that make you feel unloved, you need to take a closer look at this. What actions or behaviors make you feel loved or unloved? Let them know.

If you let them know and they continue to behave in a way you consider harmful, hurtful or injurious, perhaps you should assess the whole situation based on the signature of love.

The Signature of Love

Love leaves its signature wherever it goes. We must learn how to tell the genuine signature of love from the counterfeit.

People make many statements in the name of love. Sometimes their love is true and sometimes it is not. Anyone can say the right things to make someone else believe that they feel a certain way.

When real love is present, its attributes are also present. They are patience, kindness, non-jealousy, non-boastfulness, humility, honorability, unselfishness, not hot-tempered, does not keep score, does not delight in evil, and rejoices with the truth. Love always protects, always trusts, always hopes, and always perseveres. And love never fails.

Additionally, love is a soothing balm that brings comfort to our weary and hurting hearts and spirits. All people experience the devastations of hurt and pain within their lifetimes. We all have pain. Yet we also have a salve which soothes our hurts, pains, and deepest yearnings. That salve is love.

Sometimes we love someone and the love is not reciprocated. This hurts us deeply. But we do our best to move on beyond the pain. It is easier for some than others. But we all long to love and be loved.

Some people give up on love because they experience disappointment in their lives. They do not realize that it is not love, but people who do not understand love, who have hurt or disappointed them. They may give up on love or on a relationship. Or we may sometimes be prone to give up on love, to wonder, "Am I really loveable?"

But I want you to know that love has never given up on you. Love never quits. Love will not perish or fade. Love is a gift that will keep on giving kindness, goodness, and radiant hope into our lives. When it is true, it lasts and endures. If it does not, it was not love. No matter what comes against it, whether time or distance or life's challenges, when love is true, it remains true.

When love is true, you will feel and sense its signature on your heart and spirit.

Types of Love

There are three types of love. These are described in ancient Greek literature and culture. They are Phileo, Eros, and Agape. Phileo is friendship love. Eros is desire-based love. It is often physical, sexual, and/or possessive. Agape is spiritual love. It is the purest, deepest, most comprehensive, lasting love. It does not seek to consume or use. Rather, it seeks to contribute to one's well-being out of the wealth of its own well-being.

Agape love is the greatest gift we can ever give or receive. The most important quality of Agape love is pervasiveness. Agape love is pervasive love. It is love that does not waiver or change due to circumstances.

When I first began telling people I was writing a book on love – Agape love – they said, "Oh, that's God's love, right? He is the only one who loves perfectly."

Agape love is perfect love. But another meaning of the word perfect is complete. Agape love is complete love. It is comprehensive love. It is the most complete love in

Greek philosophy. Agape love is the love God has for us, but He also intends for it to be the love we have for Him, ourselves, and one another.

Definition of Love

So what is love, really? Love is defined as affection, good will, and benevolence.[1]

Yet when it comes to love, what convictions about love do many of us have? Most people do not know how to more deeply define or describe it. This is especially true in English. Sanskrit has 96 words for love. Ancient Persian has 80. Greek has 3. And English only 1.

The Huffington Post published an article on "96 Words for Love" which elaborates on the great need in English-speaking language and culture to communicate more deeply and comprehensively regarding love.

The author describes various feelings related to love: appreciation, comfort, gratitude, warmth, tingles, trust, awe, softness, joy, contentment, and stability.[2]

These feelings oftentimes accompany love. They are the fruits of love. But as we are about to discover in this book, they are not the only attributes. And an even more

---

[1] Strong's Concordance: 26 from ἀγάπη Transliterated: agape.

[2] Huffington Post "96 Words for Love" www.huffingtonpost.com/sheryl-paul/96-words-for-love_b_1644658.html

powerful combination of attributes associated with love will increase your experience with and ability to love others well and tell the difference between what is truly love and what is not love. We will become acquainted with these attributes shortly.

What makes them different is that these commonly associated feelings ebb and flow, wax and wane, and intensify or diminish depending on life's challenges and circumstances. However, when love is true, several key attributes are present with it.

We must learn how to recognize agape love in order to be able to discern love. We are not the only ones. People across all socioeconomic strata and backgrounds have a need to know what love is, no matter what their background is.

Ancient Understanding of Love

Almost 2,000 years ago, a letter was written which describes love's attributes comprehensively as it relates to Agape love. This letter was written by Paul of Tarsus to the people of Corinth, Greece. Like many of the world's large urban cities today, Corinth was full of all kinds of people. It was a diverse socioeconomic crossroads for trade and commerce. All kinds of people with all kinds of values and priorities came through or lived there.

Corinth was a very wealthy city. People had what they needed materially. Yet they did not always have what they needed most: true love or the truth about love. Today, many of us live in or near big cities where we can get what we need materially, also. But like the

Corinthians, even if someone's material needs are met, they still hunger for the greatest need of all: the need to love and be loved.

Paul wrote the Corinthians a letter to tell them about the importance of love, what love is, and how empty their lives would be without it, even if they had everything else they needed.

Here is the letter he wrote:

If I speak in the tongues of men and of angels, but I do not have love, I am a noisy gong or a clanging cymbal. And if I have prophecy, and know all mysteries and all knowledge, and if I have all faith so that I can remove mountains, but do not have love, I am nothing. If I give away everything I own, and if I give over my body in order to boast, but do not have love, I receive no benefit.

Love is patient, love is kind, it is not envious. Love does not brag, it is not puffed up. It is not rude, it is not self-serving, it is not easily angered or resentful. It is not glad about injustice, but rejoices in the truth. It bears all things, believes all things, hopes all things, endures all things.

Love never ends. But if there are prophecies, they will be set aside; if there are tongues, they will cease; if there is knowledge, it will be set aside. For we know in part, and we prophesy in part, but when what is perfect comes, the partial will be set aside. When I was a child, I talked like a child, I thought like a child, I reasoned like a child. But when I became an adult, I set aside childish ways. For now we see in a mirror indirectly, but then we will see face to face. Now I know in part, but then I will know fully, just as I have been fully known. And now these three remain: faith, hope, and love. But the greatest of these is love.

From 1 Corinthians 13, Net Bible (www.bible.org)

This letter makes two very important points: many people can talk about all kinds of things and make great fanfare but if they don't have love in their hearts, it is only empty chatter and noise. On the other hand, we may have great faith and even hope, but the greatest of these is love. And love never fails. It is not wishy-washy. It is consistent and always perseveres.

Attributes of The Gift

Certain attributes accompany The Gift of love. Below, you will find the attributes, their definitions, and descriptions. All attributes are taken from the original definitions of the Greek words used to describe love spoken of in the Letter to the Corinthians, Chapter 13 from the Net Bible. I use the NET Bible often in my ongoing study of biblical Greek and Hebrew because it is one of the most accurate translations and helpful online resources available. You can find the NET Bible at https://net.bible.org.

The NET Bible specializes in presenting deeper understanding of the Bible's meaning based on the original languages in which it was written. The Old Testament was written in Hebrew. The New Testament was written in Greek.

The following is a list of love's attributes as found in the Letter To The Corinthians written in AD 53-57. This letter reveals the truth about love, how to know and recognize love, and all that love is meant to be.

We know love *is love* when the following attributes are present. If they are not present, it is not love.

ATTRIBUTES OF THE GIFT OF LOVE

Patience

Love is patient.

Patient - to be of a long spirit, not to lose heart, to persevere patiently and bravely in enduring misfortunes and troubles, to be patient in bearing the offenses and injuries of others, to be mild and slow in avenging, to be longsuffering, slow to anger, slow to punish.[3]

To be patient is to hold on when you feel like giving up. It is to hold back when you feel like lashing out. It is to persevere patiently and bravely in enduring misfortunate and troubles.

Love is patient. It is not quick to punish, nor does it punish harshly. It perseveres bravely in difficult times.

Kindness

Love is kind.

---

[3] The Ancient Greek word for kindness is μακροθυμεῖ. Strong's 3116

Kindness (χρηστεύεται) – This word does not refer only to one's words and countenance. It refers to the virtue that pervades and penetrates the whole nature, that mellows anything harsh and austere. It is a virtue which is gentle and delights in encouraging others.[4]

Not Envious

Love does not envy.

Envy (ζηλοῖ) - to burn with zeal, to be heated or to boil with envy, hatred, anger

Love does not envy. It does not burn with an all-consuming passion fueled by jealousy, hatred, or anger. If a person is behaving that way toward you and calls it love, it is not love. Love is never destructive. It is life-giving. Love does not hate the one it professes to adore or favor.[5]

Not Boastful

Love does not boast.

---

[4] The Greek word for kindness is χρηστεύεται. Strong's: 5541 and 5544. Transliterated: chrēsteuetai.

[5] The Greek word for envy is ζηλοῖ. Strong's: 2206. Transliterated: zēloi Root: ζηλόω

To boast (περπερεύεται) - a self display, employing rhetorical embellishments in extolling one's self excessively.[6]

Love does not say, "Look at me!" "Look at how great I am!" If someone is bragging about his or her own accomplishments and what a great person they are, they are not doing so from a place of love.

Love is not arrogant.
Arrogant (φυσιοῦται) - to inflate, blow up, to cause to swell up, to puff up, make proud, to be puffed up, to bear one's self loftily, be proud.[7]

Love does not act arrogantly. It does not swell up with pride which says, "I am better than you!" or "I am God's gift to the world!"

Not Inappropriate

Love does not act unbecomingly or inappropriately.

To act unbecomingly (ἀσχημονεῖ) – To act unbecomingly is to act improperly or in a way that is inappropriate. It is

---

[6] The Greek word for boast is περπερεύεται.
Strong's: 4068. Transliterated: perpereuetai.

[7] The Greek word for proud/pompous is φυσιοῦται.
Strong's: 5448. Transliterated: phusioutai.

to run the risk of bringing someone into danger or disgrace.[8]

Today, more and more, people run the risk of this unloving behavior as they relate to one another in relationships as well as via social media platforms.

We must be careful not to disgrace one another, either publicly or privately. It is not loving or beneficial to anyone involved.

Not Self-Absorbed

Love is not self-absorbed.

Self-absorbed (ζητεῖ τὰ ἑαυτῆς) - to seek in order to find, to seek a thing, to seek [in order to find out] by thinking, meditating, reasoning, to enquire into, to seek after, seek for, aim at, strive after, to seek i.e. require, demand, to crave, demand something from someone.[9]

Love is not self-infatuated. Although it knows it has value, it recognizes others do, too. Love is not egotistical. It truly cares about others, not just itself. It does not seek out or strive after its own self-importance. It also recognizes the importance, significance, and contribution of others.

---

[8] The Greek word for unbecomingly is ἀσχημονεῖ. Strong's: 807. Transliterated: aschēmonei.

[9] The Greek phrase for self-absorbed/self-seeking is οὐ ζητεῖ τὰ ἑαυτῆς. Strong's: 2212. Transliterated: zētei.

Is Not Easily Angered

Love is not easily angered, exasperated or irritated.

Angered/exasperated (παροξύνεται) – to arouse to anger, exasperate, irritate, burn with anger, sharpen with contention, provoke.[10]

Love is not easily angered, exasperated, or irritated. It does not become easily enraged. One Christmas season, my daughter and I were shopping at a department store. A fancily-dressed woman stood at the cash register next to us buying luxurious throws and other Christmas gifts. Her two young children were playing with their plastic bottles of soda, tossing them in the air.

Scowling, she raised her voice and told them, "Stop that!" She continued to berate her kids, yelling at them and talking down to them in front of all the customers.

Later, my daughter commented on the woman's behavior. She said, "That lady did not seem to be in a very loving Christmas spirit, even though she was buying lots of nice presents." The truth is, love is not easily angered, exasperated or irritated.

Furthermore, love does not easily anger, exasperate or irritate. It is important to keep ourselves in check

---

[10] The Greek word for not easily angered is οὐ παροξύνεται. Strong's: 3947. Transliterated: paroxunetai.

regarding this. Anyone can fall into this trap. The woman was wearing an elaborate jeweled headband and fancy outfit, but she had forgotten to put on the most beautiful jewel: the jewel of love in her heart.

No matter what one is wearing, or what possessions one has, the greatest gift of all is love.

Does Not Make A Record of Rights and Wrongs

Love does not keep score.

Keep score (οὐ λογίζεται) – to take an inventory, to assign credit or a debt to one's account, also used in reference to balancing one's finances.[11]

Love does not keep score. How many times have we known someone who thought they gave generously but rather always kept score. "I did this for you. What have you done for me?" they say. Or perhaps we have been that person. That is not love.

Love does not keep score of debts owed, just as it does not keep a record of wrongs. Love is free-flowing and behaves more like a gentle river which flows from and through and to us with lasting strength. It does not to keep score because it does not give to get. It gives because it finds joy in giving. And it is free to do so. Love does not owe anyone anything and it does not

---

[11] The Greek word for keep score is λογίζεται. Strong's: 3049. Transliterated: logizetai.

demand anything from anyone in exchange for its fullness. Rather, it hopes, perseveres, and keeps on going.

Is Not Injurious

Love does not engage in destructive thinking, feeling, or acting.

Injurious/destructive (κακόν). - of a bad nature, not such as it ought to be, of a mode of thinking, feeling, acting, base, wrong, wicked, troublesome, injurious, pernicious, destructive, baneful.[12]

Kakos indicates the lack in a person or thing of those qualities which should be possessed and means bad in character. This includes one's moral character, way of thinking, feeling, and/or acting, and involves injurious, destructive, and malignant intent or results. It is the opposite of beneficial.

Love does not manifest itself from a place of wickedness. It does not engage in destructive thoughts. It does not operate from a base of feelings or actions which are destructive or seek to destroy. When people think, feel, or act that way, it is not love.

Does Not Rejoice In Unrighteousness/Unfairness

Love does not find joy in injustice.

---

[12] The Greek word for this is τὸ κακόν. Strong's: 2556. Transliterated: kakon.

Rejoice (χαίρει) - to rejoice, be glad, to rejoice exceedingly, to be well, thrive, in salutations, hail!, at the beginning of letters: to give one greeting, salute.

Unrighteousness/Injustice (ἀδικία) - injustice, of a judge, unrighteousness of heart and life, a deed violating law and justice, act of unrighteousness, a condition of not being right with God, humanity, or one's conscience.[13]

Love does not find joy in unfairness or injustice. When things are not right between people in relationships, it cannot rejoice. It is not glad about deeds which violate the law and justice or deeds which are not fair in general.

Equally, love does not take delight in one's violations of conscience, not being right with God, and not being right with one another. Love seeks to make things right, to make amends, and to restore relationships and goodness to its fullness inside of them.

Truth

Love rejoices in the truth.[14]

---

[13] The Greek phrase is οὐ χαίρει ἐπὶ τῇ ἀδικίᾳ. Rejoice: (χαίρει) Strong's: 5463. Transliterated: chairei. Unrighteousness: (ἀδικία) Strong's: 93. Transliterated: adikia.

[14] The Greek phrase is συγχαίρει δὲ τῇ ἀληθείᾳ.

Rejoice in/with (συγχαίρει δὲ) -- to rejoice with, take part in another's joy, to rejoice together, to congratulate.[15]

The Truth (τῇ ἀληθείᾳ) - objectively, what is true in any matter under consideration, truly, in truth, according to truth, of a truth, in reality, in fact, certainly, what is true in things appertaining to God and the duties of man, moral and religious truth, in the greatest latitude, the true notions of God which are open to human reason without His supernatural intervention, the truth as taught in the Christian religion, respecting God and the execution of his purposes through Christ, and respecting the duties of man, opposing alike to the superstitions of the Gentiles and the inventions of the Jews, and the corrupt opinions and precepts of false teachers even among Christians, subjectively, truth as a personal excellence, that candor of mind which is free from affection, pretense, simulation, falsehood, deceit.[16]

Love rejoices in the truth. It rejoices in what is sincere, earnest, real, and true which will be true in any matter under consideration. It does not rejoice in falsehood or deceit, whether by individuals or false teachers.

The truth is earnest and sincere. It is straightforward. It is not misleading. It brings with it personal excellence

---

[15] Rejoices with. συγχαίρει δὲ. Strong's: 4796. Transliterated: sunchairei.

[16]

The Truth (τῇ ἀληθείᾳ) (Strong's: 225) Transliterated: alētheia and candor of mind which is free from pretense, falsehood, and deceit.

It bears, believes, hopes, and endures.

Love bears all things, believes all things, hopes all things, endures all things.[17]

All - πάντα –all, the whole, everyone, all things, everything, collectively, thoroughly (From πασ Strong's 3956)

Love bears, supports and protects.

Supports/Protects (πάντα στέγει) - deck, thatch, to cover, to protect or keep by covering, to preserve, to cover over with silence, to keep secret, to hide, conceal, of the errors and faults of others, by covering to keep off something which threatens, to bear up against, hold out against, and so endure, bear, forbear.[18]

This word means to protect or preserve by covering. When a guy buys a fancy sports car, he will often put a cover on it to protect and preserve the paint. He does not want anything to happen to his car!

---

[17] The Greek phrase is πάντα στέγει, πάντα πιστεύει, πάντα ἐλπίζει, πάντα ὑπομένει..

[18] Greek: πάντα στέγει .Strong's: 4722. Transliterated: stegei.

Yet when it comes to people and our love for them,
whether love toward ourselves or others, how often do
we cover over one another in love intentionally? In
relationships, when people become upset with one
another, they sometimes expose one another, disgrace, or
damage one another often with words and sometimes
actions, also. Yet that is not what love does.

Love covers and preserves people to protect them. It
covers and preserved them and their dignity and
personhood as a treasure just as guys cover their sports
cars. Yet sometimes people do not take as good care of
each other in this way as they do their things.

People are more important than things and loving them
well is love's highest priority. It can be ours, too. We
must seek to receive the gift of love, learn to enjoy it, and
share it with others. In doing so, we will experience all
the fullness of joy in what love is.

Love supports and protects in all things. In other words,
it supports and protects thoroughly, not just partially or
sometimes. All means all.

Love trusts confidently and believes continuously.

Trust confidently (πάντα πιστεύει) - to think to be true, to
be persuaded of, to credit, place confidence in, of the
thing believed, to credit, have confidence, in a moral or
religious reference, used in the NT of the conviction and
trust to which a man is impelled by a certain inner and
higher prerogative and law of soul, to trust in Jesus or
God as able to aid either in obtaining or in doing
something: saving faith, mere acknowledgment of some

fact or event: intellectual faith, to entrust a thing to one, i.e. his fidelity, to be entrusted with a thing.

Love trusts confidently and thoroughly.

It trusts confidently through all times, whether good or challenging.[19]

Love hopes continuously.

Hope (ἐλπίζει) - to hope, in a religious sense, to wait for salvation with joy and full confidence, hopefully to trust in. To hope is to place an expectant confidence and trust in someone.[20]

Love remains.

To remain (ὑπομένει) - to remain, to tarry behind, to remain i.e. abide, not recede or flee, to preserve: under misfortunes and trials to hold fast to one's faith in Christ, to endure, bear bravely and calmly under suffering.[21]

Love stays. It does not abandon. It endures circumstances bravely and calmly. It bears up under

---

[19] Greek: πάντα πιστεύει. Strong's: 4100. Transliterated: pisteuei Root: πιστεύω.

[20] Greek: ἐλπίζει. Strong's: 1679. Transliterated: elpizei.

[21] Greek: ὑπομένει. Strong's: 5278. Transliterated: hupomenei. Root: ὑπομένω.

painful circumstances and perseveres. It stays under misfortunes and trials. It abides.

To abide is to wait, to remain as one, to be present and to continue to be present. Love does not go away. It stays with its beloved.

Love never fails or ends.[22]

Never: (οὐδέποτε) – Never means never

Fails/ends (πίπτει) - to fall down, fall into ruin, to descend from a higher place to a lower, to fall (either from or upon), to be thrust down, metaph. to fall under judgment, came under condemnation, to descend from higher position, of those overcome by terror or astonishment or grief, fall into ruin: of buildings, walls etc., to be cast down from a state of prosperity, to fall from a state of uprightness, to perish, i.e. come to an end, disappear, cease, of virtues, to lose authority, no longer have force, of sayings, precepts, etc., to be removed from power by death, to fail of participating in, miss a share in.[23]

Never means never. Love never, ever ends. It is never overcome by fear. It never falls and never fails. It never ceases of its virtues. It never loses authority. It never stops being the powerful force that it is. It cannot be removed from power by death.

---

[22] The Greek Phrase is Ἡ ἀγάπη οὐδέποτε πίπτει.

[23] Greek: πίπτει. Strong's: 4098. Transliterated: piptei.

In short, nothing can stop love!

Love exhibits these qualities. When love takes hold of our hearts, deep and pervasive love, these qualities will persevere. Love is consistent. It is trustable, reliable, dependable, and you can count on it. When a person loves with these qualities, you don't have to question them.

Love Holds Its Own

In sum, love holds its own. So we must learn to hold fast to love and its attributes in our own hearts, minds, and lives.

When love is true, it is consistent. Many people misunderstand love because they experience love's attributes inconsistently from some who claim to love but do not know how to truly love.

Love cannot be manipulated, controlled, forced, coerced, or demanded to be present and give of itself. And anyone who would demand that is not loving. It either is or is not.

Love Is Supernatural

We desire to love well. Sometimes we are hard on ourselves or others in regard to love because we try to love well but sometimes it feels like we just are not able! However, love does not come naturally. Rather, it is supernatural. It is a gift which comes from God and is sustained by His supernatural ability, power, wisdom, and strength. It is sustained by His grace, which is His unmerited favor toward us.

Love is a supernatural gift. And even receiving and giving love is a supernatural act. Something that is supernatural is beyond us, from the higher spiritual realm of heaven. And every good and perfect gift comes from God. Love is the perfect gift. Love comes from God. In fact, love is the gift God gives to us – every day in a multitude of ways.

Have you ever felt like someone showed you kindness? Or blessed you with goodness? Their very ability and propensity to do that came from God. It was given to them by God, whether they recognize or acknowledge His direct involvement.

Here is why: Love is from God. And it is also the essence of who God is. So all love is from God.

Wounds from Unloving

When people think, speak, and act in ways that are unloving, it wounds. We wound others and others wound us in these ways. Many people harbor and nurture love wounds for days, months, and years. Before they know it, years of their life have passed so quickly. Yet they still bear the same wounds they did so many years ago.

Others become determined to find healing, hope, and a future beyond their love wounds. They go on to have more satisfying, fulfilling, and meaningful lives, often infused with love, hope and joy.

Whether a person languishes in love wounds or lives beyond them into a life of love's victories depends not on love or opportunity but on the individual's decision. Love is strong enough to get us through, over, and beyond anything. We just must embrace it!

A Prayer for You:

"I pray that out of his glorious riches he may strengthen you with power through his Spirit in your inner being, so that Christ may dwell in your hearts through faith. And I pray that you, being rooted and established in love, may have power, together with all the Lord's holy people, to grasp how wide and long and high and deep is the love of Christ, and to know this love that surpasses knowledge— that you may be filled to the measure of all the fullness of God."

Ephesians 3:16-19

PART 2. RECEIVING THE GIFT

We all find ourselves in different places when it comes to our love journey.

Do you believe love is real?

Love is real! We just must learn to embrace it. We must learn to receive love.

Do you believe that you can love and be loved? Some people do. Some people don't.

Some people yearn to be loved but do not believe that others will find them truly loveable. Others believe they are lovable and that the world should love them, but they are not as good at loving others as they are loving themselves.

I want you to know that you are loveable. Take a moment to tell yourself, "I am loveable." Take a moment to let it sink in. Then say it again. And again. "I am loveable."

The way to ever have love or give love is to receive love first. We cannot give something that we do not have. That would be impossible. And since love is supernatural, it comes from God and we must receive it from Him and let His love live in us in order to be able to give it to others and to discern it in others.

Each person has a choice what they will do with love. But the most important choice we must make is to first receive love ourselves. We can only give what we have. If we have love, we will give love. If we don't have it, then we cannot give it. Rather, we will give a counterfeit affection we call love. But when we put its attributes to the test (of the signature and attributes of love discussed above), it will not pass the test.

If these attributes are present, it is love. When people love one another, they do not merely try or wish to live lovingly. Rather, their relationships bear the signature of love. This is true whether it is a romantic relationship, friends, family, acquaintances, or our relationship with God. Love is love. We all must work on being about love intentionally and consistently in all of our relationships. In order to do so, we must be intentional about being rooted in love. To be rooted in love, we must open our hearts to receive the gift of love.

Rooted In Love

The Gift of love has many attributes and it compels us to let them take root in our hearts. I have found it helpful to pray and ask God to give me a nudge on my heart to help me know which attributes to especially focus on in my personal growth. I encourage you to do the same.

When love is present in its fullness, it displays all of these qualities. And it does so with gentle and pervasive persistence.

If you desire to grow in love and you find yourself having self-condemning thoughts, these are not the voice of love. Love does not condemn or tear down. It is not harsh or caustic. It is gentle, patient, and kind.

If people have been telling you that you are not loving, ask God to help you become more loving. And ask God to show you the truth about what they are saying. I also encourage and invite you to pray that those you know would also become more loving and that they, too, would persevere in love.

Sometimes we find it is easy to be loving for a moment or a season, but when love is true, it is also deep – deeper than the challenges and circumstances that come against it. If a tree has strong roots and it is planted securely in the ground, when windstorms come against it, it may bend but it will not break. It can be a relatively thin tree or delicate tree, even. But when it is securely rooted, it will stand against many tests.

When a person determines to be rooted in love, they, too, will be like the tree. They may bend but they will not break when challenging circumstances or destructive forces come into their life.

It is equally important to persevere in love and to let it root itself in us, in our hearts, minds, and souls. If you open your heart to love's attributes, they will grow in you. As a flower blooms and keeps blooming, love's attributes desire to bloom in us. They are the fragrance of love. And it is love's desire that they would be ever-present in us. We must actively seek to grow in love and allow love to root itself deeply in us.

Meditation

An ancient tradition I find helps me grow my heart and mind in love is meditation. People have been meditation for thousands of years. Many meditation practices exist across various peoples and cultures. I prefer the Christian meditation tradition because it connects me to the Maker and Giver of Perfect Love.

To meditate is to center our mind, heart, and spirit on love – and on God -- and in doing so, allow ourselves to open up more fully to love.

Some people call meditation "mindfulness" because it requires focusing our minds. Our minds can be pulled in so many directions. Many distractions compete for our attention. But we must learn to be attentive to what is most important.

Meditation is an exercise and positive discipline that centers, fills, and satiates our minds and hearts. It is not only mind and logic-centered, but heart, feeling, and spirit-centered as well.

We were given both thoughts and feelings for a reason. We must learn how to listen to and abide with both. Doing so helps us be more discerning in our own lives and in relating to others.

Take 5-10 minutes to practice this prayer meditation. As you learn how to center your mind and heart on love, you will grow more deeply in your own ability to receive and give love.

Meditation Exercise:

1. Go into a quiet place (a room, closet, other quiet space)
2. Sit upright in a comfortable chair with your feet on the floor.

3. Take deep breaths, slowly breathing in through your nose and out through your mouth.
4. Sit with your hands resting comfortably on your lap with palms facing down or up. (Choose whichever you prefer.)
5. As you take slow, deep breaths, focus on breathing in love and breathing out un-love. Focus on allowing love to fill you and ridding yourself of unlove (whether your own or someone else's doing).
6. Do this for 5-10 minutes. Set a timer which will chime gently when finished if needed.
7. Focus by thinking or saying any or all of the following: "I am loveable. I receive love. I expel all unlovingness. I center myself in love. I will receive love and be a giver of love."
8. As you finish, sit quietly for 1-2 minutes, paying attention to how you are feeling. Mindfully observe (pay attention to) what and how you are feeling. Did the meditation draw you deeper into love? If yes, then allow yourself to feel, enjoy, and rest in the joy of going deeper in love. If not, with compassion on yourself, assess why not. Were your thoughts restless? Did you have trouble focusing? Is something distracting or troubling you? Say what it is and then, whether now or later, sit down to meditate again.

Meditation Using Prayer Beads

Here is another meditation exercise you can try if you have prayer beads. For my meditation, I use Anglican prayer beads. For more information on prayer beads and where to buy them, see www.AmandaJSeymour.com

1. Go into a quiet place (a room, closet, other quiet space)
2. Sit upright in a comfortable chair with your feet on the floor.
3. Take deep breaths, slowly breathing in through your nose and out through your mouth.
4. Sit with your hands resting comfortably on your lap holding a set of prayer beads gently in your hands.
5. As you take slow, deep breaths, focus on breathing in love and breathing out un-love. Focus on allowing love to fill you and ridding yourself of unlove (whether your own or someone else's doing).
6. Pray the "ACTS" Prayer. ACTS stands for Adoration, Confession, Thanksgiving, Supplication. Sit quietly. Move gently from bead to bead, starting with the cross. Pray "Thank you for love. I receive Your Perfect Love." Move to the first bead. Pray "Thank you for loving me, Lord."   Allow yourself to feel His love enveloping you and filling your heart, bringing confidence to your mind, and strengthening your spirit.

7. Next, pray the ACTS prayer, moving along each bead as you pray:

   A-Adoration: Tell God 7 attributes you appreciate about Him and what you appreciate about love.

C-Confession: Confess 7 things you know you have done to not love God, yourself, or others fully.

T-Thanksgiving: Thank God for 7 blessings related to love.

S-Supplication: Request God's help for 7 concerns related to love.

8. As you finish, sit quietly for 1-2 minutes, paying attention to how you are feeling. Mindfully observe (pay attention to) what and how you are feeling. Did the meditation draw you deeper into love? If yes, then allow yourself to feel, enjoy, and rest in the joy of going deeper in love. If not, with compassion on yourself, assess why not. Were your thoughts restless? Did you have trouble focusing? Is something distracting or troubling you? Say what it is and then, whether now or later, sit down to meditate again.

Meditation is beautiful and powerful in that it will help you become rooted in love. It will also grow your love and connection to God and His love. His love is the love from which all true love flows, whether our love for God or love for one another, whether in romantic relationships, friendships, family, community, acquaintances, or any other relationship.

The truth is, we must *learn* to receive love and to give love to others. If love came naturally, don't you think everyone would love so much better and more fully than we sometimes do or feel we should?

The best way to learn to love is to learn to become rooted in love. Regarding being rooted and established in love, Paul wrote a letter to the people of Ephesus, Turkey, encouraging them in this.

He wrote:

"I pray that out of His glorious riches He may strengthen you with power through His Spirit in your inner being, so that Christ may dwell in your hearts through faith. And I pray that you, being rooted and established in love, may have power, together with all the Lord's holy people, to grasp how wide and long and high and deep is the love of Christ, and to know this love that surpasses knowledge—that you may be filled to the measure of all the fullness of God."[24]

Ellicott's Commentary For English Readers Ephesians 3:17 describes being rooted in love:

Rooted.—We cast our affections down into the character and the Being of God; we wind them about His attributes; we strike them into His promises; we drive them deep into His faithfulness. There the roots of our affection lie. They take up, they drink in, the nature of the love they live in; they are always assimilating themselves to it, and they send up its sweet savour by little, silent threads, which are always running to the fountain of life. Our words, our actions, our whole outer being, cannot choose but mould itself to them, and take that love. Because of those secret processes of the roots which are

---

[24] Letter To The Ephesians 3:16-19

in Christ, we love. We love simply because we are rooted in love.

Most men, when they wish to be religious, begin by trying to give up certain things, and to do certain other actions. But there must be something that goes before that, else it is just as if you planted leaves without stems, or flowers without roots. The springs of life must be in their right places. The roots must be really in God. True religion does not consist so much in this thing, or that thing, as being always in a certain tone and atmosphere. The plant takes its character from the ground; the soul, from its inmost, deepest associations. There must be that behind whereby we are always making inspirations of love.[25]

The fullness spoken of here refers to the presence of God, His power, and His fullness like a ship is full of oarsmen and sailors. Jesus is present with us, and He is the captain of our souls and our love. May we let His love overtake us and drive us on in victory in our lives!

Prior to being able to love others well, we must learn to love ourselves. This takes intentionality and practice. But it can be done. Anything can be achieved with intentionality and practice.

Love Yourself

If we are to love others well, we must first learn how to love ourselves. Love has many facets. Just as a diamond

---

[25] Ellicott's Commentary For English Readers Ephesians 3:17

has many faces, love has many attributes. It is a supernatural wonder which, throughout time, has somehow seemingly become commonplace.

In order to love well and fully, we must be intentional about applying the Attributes of Love toward ourselves.

Apply the attributes of love to yourself and your own life first. Make decisions that protect your well-being and the well-being of others. Treat yourself with patience, kindness, non-boastfulness, humility, honorability, and unselfishness. Do not delight in evil, rejoice with the truth. Believe that love can and will triumph over fear, self-doubt, jealousy and strife. And then let it do so. Let yourself be full of hope, and persevere in love. Know that love will not fail you, abandon you, or reject you. Love will always be for you.

The Greatest Love

The greatest love is found in Jesus Christ. Jesus Christ, is God's only begotten son, which means He is the only one who has ever been born directly from God the Father. As God the Father is love, so Jesus The Christ is also love.

God demonstrated His great love for us in this: while we were yet sinners, (that is, wrongdoers), Christ died for us. And we love because He first loved us.[26]

1 John 4:19 says:

---

[26] 1 John 4:19

49

We love because he loved us first.

If anyone says "I love God" and yet hates his fellow Christian, he is a liar, because the one who does not love his fellow Christian whom he has seen cannot love God whom he has not seen. And the commandment we have from him is this: that the one who loves God should love his fellow Christian too.

If you are going to receive The Gift, you must believe you can. Do you believe you are lovable? If not, I am here to tell you that you *are* loveable! And I will believe for you until you fully believe it if you don't already!

Do you believe you can love others well? If not, I am here to tell you that you can! Give your heart to God and His love and He will give His love to you!

Pray:

Lord, thank You for loving me. Thank You that I am loveable! I give You my heart and ask You to fill it with Your love. I desire to receive Your love so that I may love You, myself, and others well. In Jesus' name. Amen.

PART 3. GIVING THE GIFT

Now that we know more about what love is and how to receive it, the question remains, how do we love? How do we give the gift of love? Sometimes people focus so much on whether or not they have received love, they tend to forget about the privilege of giving love.

If we are going to love well, we must first believe that we can. The wisest approach to loving well is to ask the one who is love and who gives all love to strengthen us with His love and to even love through us.

Our hearts are like a throne from which we direct our lives through our hearts. When we ask Jesus Christ to be the Lord of our hearts and lives and to sit on the throne of our hearts, something amazing and wonderful happens. He gives us all the love we need to love with Pervasive Love, His love. He directs our hearts and loves through us.

The best way to love is to be intentional about it. We must make time to be attentive in love toward others. I find it helpful to place reminders around my home, office, and workspace to motivate and encourage me to persevere in the courage it takes to love, be vulnerable, and go for my dreams. I have placed motivational magnets on a clipboard with these phrases:

*Proceed as if success is inevitable.

*To the world you may be one person, but to one person you may be the world.

*Life does not have to be perfect to be wonderful.

*Life begins at the end of your comfort zone.

*Twenty years from now you will be more disappointed by the things you didn't do than by the ones you did. So throw off the bowlines. Sail away from the safe harbor. Catch the trade winds in your sails. Explore. Dream. Discover.

It helps to cheer ourselves and others on in love.

The Gift of Pervasive Love

To give the gift of love well, we must give it securely and pervasively. Loving others can make us feel vulnerable. Yet just as roots of a tree implant themselves in ground securely and pervasively, we must root ourselves in love and allow our rootedness to help us feel and be secure in love.

We must also focus on being pervasive, persistent, and consistent in our lovingness. When love is true, it is also pervasive, consistent, and persistent. If someone says they love you and they are loving one minute and cruel the next, that is not love.

Our hearts encounter stumbling blocks regarding love when we meet people who do not believe they can love God, themselves, or others consistently, pervasively, and comprehensively. Rather, they express love to some people sometimes and others at other times. But sometimes they are loving and good to acquaintances and strangers, people in public, but they do not treat those closest to them with the same love and goodwill. This is not love. We must learn to discern love from unlove.

Doing so will help us get involved and invested in healthy relationships and dislodge and cut off unhealthy ones.

True love is the same in public and in private. It is consistent and pervasive. It is something we must learn and we can learn in order to live a more fulfilling and inspired life.

Once we learn how to live in love pervasively, we will forever possess the key to true peace, joy, contentment and fulfillment. Until we learn how to live in pervasive love, we will not.

The most impactful place to start in giving pervasive love is to the One who gave us love in the first place.

Loving God

We love because God first loved us. (1 John 4:19) God is love. In Him, there is no darkness at all, no despair, no lack of hope. The attributes of love are the attributes of God, and they are made visible to us in Jesus Christ.

To know what God is like, insert "God" into this description on love, for God and love are one.

The Way of Love

If I speak in the tongues of men and of angels, but I do not have **love**, I am a noisy gong or a clanging cymbal. And if I have prophecy, and know all mysteries and all knowledge, and if I have all faith so that I can remove mountains, but do not have **love**, I am nothing. If I give away everything I own, and if I give over my body in order to boast, but do not have **love**, I receive no benefit.

Love is patient, love is kind, it is not envious. **Love** does not brag, it is not puffed up. It is not rude, it is not self-serving, it is not easily angered or resentful. It is not glad about injustice, but rejoices in the truth. It bears all things, believes all things, hopes all things, endures all things.

Love never ends. But if there are prophecies, they will be set aside; if there are tongues, they will cease; if there is knowledge, it will be set aside. For we know in part, and we prophesy in part, but when what is perfect comes, the partial will be set aside. When I was a child, I talked like a child, I thought like a child, I reasoned like a child. But when I became an adult, I set aside childish ways. For now we see in a mirror indirectly, but then we will see face to face. Now I know in part, but then I will know fully, just as I have been fully known. And now these three remain: faith, hope, and **love**. But the greatest of these is **love**.[27]

The Gift Giver

The gift of love comes from heaven, from God Himself, through Jesus The Christ.

More than two-thousand years ago, Jesus The Christ died on the cross for the sin of humankind. His great love

---

[27] 1 Corinthians 13

overpowered the darkness of sin, hopelessness, lovelessness, and despair.

In His death, He triumphed over sin, death, hell and the grave. His sacrificial death paid a one-time price for the sin of humankind. And it paved the way to eternal life for all those who believe in Him, that He is who He says He is: Jesus The Christ, the anointed one who came to save us from eternal separation from God.

In His great love for us, Christ died for us. And He was raised to newness of life on the third day. He was resurrected from the grave and raised to new life. He ascended to heaven and is seated at the right hand of The Father.

Christ sent us the Holy Spirit who ministers Christ's ministry to us on earth. The Holy Spirit is our Counselor and helps us to know and do Christ's will and work. His greatest desire is that we love God and love one another.

This is why Christ told us the first and greatest commandment is to love God with all of our hearts, soul, mind, and strength. And the second commandment is to love our neighbors as ourselves.

We love because He first loved us. Even before you were born, you and I were loved.

Time With God

The first person whom we ought to love is God. I find that the most helpful way for me to do that is to spend 5-10 minutes each day reading and meditating on who God is and how He is involved in our lives. My devotional time is my time with God. It keeps me centered on God and helps me to put loving Him first.

Some of the devotionals I have enjoyed through the years include:

The Upper Room (http://devotional.upperroom.org) and *My Utmost For His Highest* (https://utmost.org).

We must also be intentional about giving love to ourselves. Some people are harder on themselves than others. But love does not treat people harshly. It does not seek to insult, tear down, or condemn. So we should not do so either, not to ourselves or others.

Lastly, we must be intentional about giving love to others. Love is a gift. It is a gift of grace. Grace is unmerited favor. Therefore, it is a gift that is not given based on whether the recipient has done something to earn it. Rather, love is a gift. It gives freely of itself without keeping score.

This is challenging for some people. We want to be remembered and appreciated for what we do and give.

Yet this is also why it is important to invest in relationships in which love is mutually expressed and experienced.

When it comes to family – the families we are born into – or families we merge with through marriage, love can be put to the test. Unlike non-familial relationships, we do not have the ability to choose who will be in our families.

So we must learn to love them even when people are very different or unappreciative toward us.

Forgiveness

Sometimes the fullest love we can extend to others also involves and requires the gift of forgiveness for love to be as pervasive as possible in the relationship. Forgiveness is love's shadow. At times, when we do not feel we can easily embrace someone in love, we must embrace them in forgiveness.

Yet learning what forgiveness is and how to forgive is a book in itself. Find out more about forgiveness in this book's sequel, *Love Beyond Measure* at www.AmandaJSeymour.com.

Suffice it to say that forgiveness is very important. And if you can't love them easily, you probably need to forgive them. To forgive is to let go of the hurts they caused.

In some cases, you may have hurt someone and need to ask their forgiveness in order to be able to move on in your love journey. Forgiving those we need to forgive frees us to love more fully. When we let go of hurts and pain and put them in the past, we free up our hands and hearts to cling to love. And we free up our attention to focus on the present and future ahead of us.

As we travel on our love journeys, we can also find ourselves surprised by love.

Surprised By Love

Each day, I am intentional about showing and expressing love and lovingness in my family. One day, my precious 10-year-old daughter decided to return the favor. She told me she had a "big surprise" planned. Mother's Day and my birthday had passed. But she said this surprise was even bigger. And it was.

Six months prior, I had lost my job. I had been working for a company that decided to shut down my department. When it happened, I became determined to work on being the best me I could be, and bring more love, joy, and fulfillment into every area of my life. This included my family, my home, entrepreneurial pursuits, and increasing our quality of life.

It also included taking my cluttered house and making it a more inviting home, which involved reading Good Housekeeping, a small book on de-cluttering, and a large 500-page book on comprehensive home cleaning. I became determined to finish projects I had started. And I always made sure we had a delicious meal and dessert to eat along the way.

Unbeknownst to me, my daughter had witnessed my determination and transformation in all of these areas. She wanted to do something special to celebrate me for it.

When the big day arrived, she told me to sleep in. So I did, which is a luxury in itself for any mom. She came into my room wearing a beautiful pink dress accompanied by the dog and cat. The cat wore a big pink, glittery bow around her neck. She made the dog a pink tie which said, "Best Mom Ever".

"Happy Mom Day!" she said. It was a Mother's Day celebration times 10. I asked her why she planned this special day. She said, "Because I love you and I am so proud of you and all that you have accomplished. I want to celebrate you!"

Then she gave me two beautiful handmade cards. The first was a "Certificate of Cleaning". It said, "You have accomplished the class called the wonderful work of cleaning and have completed the advanced level of cleaning!" Signed; Sarah.

The second card read," Ms. Seymour has shown and done great things throughout the year, and I would like to compliment them. She has shown and done:

- Determination
- Perseverance
- Trust in God
- Wisdom
- Courage
- Patience
- Cleaning
- Hard Work
- The most important thing: Love
- And much more!

Since that day, I have proudly displayed those two cards on my refrigerator so I can see and be encouraged by them every day.

My daughter prepared a delicious breakfast of fresh coffee, eggs, and crepes with Nutella. She curtsied in her fancy dress and draped a cloth napkin over her arm and curtsied as she served my breakfast.

I gave her a big hug and kiss and said, 'Thank you so much. This is wonderful!" She said, "This isn't all. The best is yet to come!"

The day before, she had spent 5 hours working on a special surprise in the kitchen the day before. She said, "Don't look! It's a surprise!"

That afternoon, she gave me a spa treatment, replete with aromatherapy, relaxing music, and a foot massage. She kept telling me all day to "*Relax!*" So I did. And I enjoyed every minute of it. With my dad's help, she even made a scrumptious dinner.

The moment for the big surprise finally arrived. "Are you ready for your big surprise?" she asked. "Yes!" I said. What happened next will forever be emblazoned on my heart and mind.

In the next moment, Sarah came around the corner singing "Happy mom day to you!" while carrying the most beautiful cake I had ever seen. She had made a 3-layer deep, dark chocolate cake with pink, purple, blue, and white frosting. It was adorned with roses, edible purple butterflies and glittery sugar sprinkles. She had made plaques out of fondant which said, "Best Mom Ever!" on the top and "Determination" and "Perseverance" on the side. She topped it with pink candles that shone in a blaze of glory, illuminating her bright smile and radiant joy as she brought it to me.

The joy in her heart and her radiant spirit and sweet love were even more beautiful than her culinary masterpiece. And the amazing thing was that prior to this, she had never made a cake except for once before and it was just a cake mix from a box with canned frosting.

That day, I was surprised by love. Love, sweet love. My daughter blessed me with her special cards, meals, spa treatment, and masterpiece cake of love. But the greatest gift of all was – and always is -- the love in her heart. It is her love that made all these wonders possible. And love is the greatest blessing of all.

We have heard time and time again that we should love one another and love God with all our heart, soul, mind, and strength. Everyone tells us to love. But moments like these remind me of the most important truth of love: It is not something that we can earn or deserve or that others can earn or deserve. Rather it is a gift. It is always a gift and only a gift.

Sometimes I meet people some days I meet people who tell me that they're just going through the motions of their life day today, just getting by to get by. Yet if we go through the motions of our lives without the gift of love at the center, without placing the gift of love at the center, then they become empty. We were not made to live that way. We were made for love. We were made to love and be loved.

We must choose to love and to love well. We must be intentional about it. And we must know that even if no one around us is cheering us on to do so, every day and every way we love and strive to love deeply and fully counts.

When we choose to live by love, we also find that we are surprised by love, delighted by love, and our lives radiate love more fully. And this is not some Pollyanna dream. Rather, it is supposed to be our most ever present and foundational reality.

The First Letter To The Corinthians Chapter 13 says that without love someone is only a clanging symbol or empty noise. People would often go to the temple in ancient Greece and make a big ruckus and fanfare during worship, but their hearts were void of love. It is possible for people to do the same, whether us or others, relating to God or one another.

But love does not pretend. It just is or is not. This is why the ancient Scriptures say, "Dear children, let us not love with words or speech but with actions and in truth."[28] Don't just say it; mean it.

When love is a gift is given in full it is the most beautiful experience, wonder, and gift anyone could ever give or receive. We must learn to enjoy it.

---

[28] 1 John 3:18

PART 4: ENJOYING THE GIFT

Can you think of a time when you truly enjoyed something – or someone? Perhaps it was a delicious meal, good music, a walk through the splendor of nature, or a memorable evening with family or friends.
In the hustle and bustle of life, it is easy to get caught up in the flurry of demands around us. In doing so, we forget to take time to *enjoy* our lives and those around us.

Learning How To Value Others

If we are to love fully, we must learn to see and value the preciousness in others, God, and ourselves. We were created for embracing the preciousness in God, ourselves and others and learning to cherish it. We were also created for community. We must be intentional about participating and investing in community.

For several years, I lived a fairly isolated life. Although I spent time with my family, I protected my heart and guarded against the vulnerability from intentionally building community and relationships in Christian community. As a single mom who was divorced and yet had a heart to love and serve the Lord, I found myself thinking, "Who would want to have me in their community? Most people –whether in the church or community in general -- only want to be friends and have fellowship with people who are married or have picture-perfect lives or are the epitome of success. I know God and my girls love me, but I am not so sure about other people!

Yet I earnestly desired fellowship – good, love-centered, healthy God-honoring, restorative and supportive relationships with other women and men as well. God knew this, so one day, He called me out of my isolation. He put a prompt in my heart to get be intentional about getting involved in community and to cast my fears aside and just go for it!

I went to a Singles event at a local church secretly hoping to meet my soulmate. But God's knowledge and timing is perfect. And He knew what I really needed was a group of solid Christ-seeking, love-rooted women in my life. A lady from Kenya named Stella was leading the group. She was very friendly and welcomed me – not just with words, but with her heart and spirit. I could feel her love. I felt invited and welcomed into the group by her lovingness.

So I went to a women's small group – after almost 10 years of feeling like a woman with no place in the church.

The Enemy of our souls, Satan, seeks to kill, steal, and destroy.[29] He wants to destroy our dreams, hope, and belief that we can ever love or be loved fully. But he is a thief and a liar, and that is all he is.

God is so much more. We must learn to listen to Him. And to know that His timing is perfect. It may not be our timing, but it is always perfect.

In His perfect timing, He brought me into community – love-centered, love-rooted community – with some of the dearest, most precious women I could have ever imagined in my life. It is an honor to love and be loved by them.

---

[29] John 10:10 "The thief comes only to steal and kill and destroy; I have come that they may have life, and have it to the full."

In time, God gave me an opportunity to come along Stella as a co-leader in our group. We meet weekly to uphold, support, and encourage one another in Christ's love and Truth in His Word.

I want to encourage you to pray for and seek the same: a love-centered, love-rooted community where you can bloom where you have been planted in your life, love, and be loved. You will know it is the right place for you because the people in the group will regard you as precious, precious to God and to them. They will echo what God says about you: You are loveable! They will appreciate and value you for who you are and your love for them. You don't or won't have to be someone you are not. You won't have to impress them. You will only need to love and be loved with a love marked by the attributes of 1 Corinthians 13.

Ecclesiastes 3:1 says, "To everything there is a season, and a time to every purpose under the heaven."

In Biblical Hebrew, the word purpose is *chapats*, which means to delight or take pleasure in. Our very purpose is to delight or take pleasure in people – in God, ourselves, and others, throughout our entire lives and theirs.

According to bible scholar Chaim Bentorah, the most accurate translation of this Ecclesiastes 3:1 is, "To all old men and the passing of time there is preciousness under heaven."[30] In other words, another way of saying this is,

---

[30] See *Hebrew Word Study: A Hebrew Teacher Finds Rest In The Heart of God* p. 44.

To all people – even into their later years in life – and the passing of time – there is preciousness under heaven. To live out our purpose to cherish and delight in the preciousness of one another, we must learn to see one another as precious.

When we learn to enjoy the gift of love in community, in our families, with friends, and extend it in daily-life to those who cross our paths, it adds a blessing, beauty, and inspiration to life that cannot be replaced or outdone by anything else and adds value to everything else.

Take Time To Love

To enjoy love to the fullest, we must take time to love. We must take time to allow ourselves to pause in the moment and become caught up in the preciousness of those around us. We can interweave and incorporate those moments into our lives. After all, they only take a moment! And doing so can make our day!

Everyone wishes they had more time in their day and their lives. I am an author, public, professor, entrepreneur, mother, and homemaker. I can keep myself busy all day long with many responsibilities. Yet I find that the only way to experience true and lasting meaning and fulfillment in my life happens when I make time to love, to be intentional about giving and enjoying love.

Without love, responsibilities are just responsibilities. Duties are just duties. Roles are just roles. But with love, everything takes on a hue of sacredness. Life becomes inspired. And with love, other good fruits grow as well, including joy, peace, patience, kindness, gentleness, and self-control.

Quality Time

Each morning, I awake at 5:30 a.m. and make coffee. I get back in bed and enjoy a cup as I read my daily devotional in *My Utmost For His Highest*. Shortly after, my young daughter awakens and climbs into my bed. I talk to her, tickle her, tell her how much I love her, and play with her. We read a book together. And I snuggle with her and hold her in my arms.

Each day, my daughters and I take time to enjoy a homemade dinner, fun crafts and activities, and being together. Many nights, she also asks me to play tag. We are very intentional about this. We call it our "quality time". We enjoy doing many things together. But most of all, we enjoy being together.

One day, I asked my older daughter, "What do you enjoy most in our life?" I thought she might say our meal times together, playing tag, or some other fun activity. Instead, she said, "I enjoy you, Grandad, the dog..."

Her answer both surprised and delighted me.

What's most enjoyable in life? It's not what we are doing or the stuff we have. It's each other!

Each day, I carve out 20-45 minutes before her bedtime that we spend doing something together that she enjoys. We play games, tag, sports, we read, enjoy a cup of non-caffeinated tea, and just enjoy being together.

We do all kinds of other things during the day before and after school. But quality time is different. It is a time when I focus my attention solely on her, not on her and on the five-hundred other things I am doing.

"I don't have time for quality time!" you might be saying. But we *must make time*. Making time for these precious love moments is one of the most important tasks we can achieve each day.

It is understandable people may feel they do not have the time. Not just individuals, but families, too. We get so busy being about our lives and various pressing demands of home, work, school, and our communities that we forget to be about each other.

I have students and adults alike who tell me that they spend several hours a day on social media, on their smart phones, laptops, and video games. Virtual reality may be appealing, informative, and interesting. It has its place as a valuable information source and a medium through which we can become more interconnected with each other through virtual means. But it will never adequately substitute for real life together time -- quality time.

What makes quality time quality is the substance of our hearts. When we are intentional and committed to giving love a prominent place in our hearts toward God, ourselves, and others, we will have the greatest gift of all time to share with others.

Learning to be attentive to the preciousness in others and creating love moments are two ways to invite pervasive love into our lives.

I have a plaque in my home which says, "Enjoy the little things in life…for one day you will look back and realize they were the big things." I keep it in a prominent place in my home as a daily reminder. It is true. The little things are often the big things. But we do not always realize it in the moment.

Learning this has given me a new perspective on life and love. The Gift of Love often expresses itself in the little things. We must learn to pay attention to and enjoy the little things more in our lives.

Taking a moment to pause, cherish, and enjoy them will amplify the radiance and impact of love in our lives. In short, doing so will make us more in touch with love. Love is all around us. We just need to be more intentional about seeing it, enjoying it, and sharing it. A kind word, a sweet kiss from a loved one or one's children, a tender embrace, and quiet moments just enjoying one another's company are all small glimmers of love in our lives. But the greatest gift of love isn't found in things. It is found in people. And it is found in the way we love.

Love Begets Love

As we learn to live and grow in love, we must remember that love begets love. When we love, love spreads. It is like a beautiful, supernatural wildfire of the heart. It is contagious. It is ongoing. Yet instead of bringing destruction, it brings restoration, life and more love!

For many years, I have been striving to be a good mom and provide a good life for my girls. Years ago, I was in an abusive marriage. And when my marriage ended, I resolved that I was never going to let anyone steal my joy and I was going to live a life intentionally focused on bringing love and infused with love and joy into every day. I had a vision for what I wanted for my daughter and myself too. No matter how difficult things became, I have always been determined to live into this every single day to the best of my ability.

I firmly believe that when parents are happy, children are happy. When parents are fulfilled, children are fulfilled. He things in life are caught just as much as they are taught and I think they are learned more fully when we exemplify them and live them rather than just telling someone else to do so. I'm a college professor. I teach a class on student success. I tell my students that everything I am teaching them I, too, am striving to live and apply in my own life each day.

One of my most prized possessions is not something elaborate or expensive. Rather, it is a small, handcrafted bookmark my daughter made for me when she was in kindergarten.

It says,

"Love is the thing that makes our hearts grow. But yours is the bigist (biggest)."

I am so grateful my sweet daughter feels that way. And I want her to always feel that way. I am very intentional about showing my love for her in ways that matter to both of us, but especially to her. I want everyone in my life to be touched by love. There is no greater gift I could ever give them.

The greatest gift anyone can give or receive is love. It is the gift that, when given, to God, ourselves or others, makes the greatest difference.

I also have a poem on my refrigerator that talks about how we handle life and how our responses to life impact our children.

Here it is:

When You Thought I Wasn't Looking

When you thought I wasn't looking,
I saw you hang my first painting on the refrigerator,
and I wanted to paint another one.

When you thought I wasn't looking,
I saw you feed a stray cat,
and I thought it was good to be kind to animals.

When you thought I wasn't looking,
I saw you make my favorite cake for me,
and I knew that little things are special things.

When you thought I wasn't looking,
I heard you say a prayer,
and I believed that there was a God to talk to.

When you thought I wasn't looking,
I felt you kiss me goodnight,

and I felt loved.

When you thought I wasn't looking,
I saw tears come from your eyes,
and I learned that sometimes things hurt,
but it's alright to cry.

When you thought I wasn't looking,
I saw that you cared,
and I wanted to be everything that I could be.

When you thought I wasn't looking,
I looked....
and I wanted to say thanks for all the things
I saw when you thought I wasn't looking.

Author: Mary Rita Schilke Korazan

I keep this poem on my refrigerator and I keep it in mind
daily.

I believe that surrounding ourselves with motivational
and inspirational reminders motivates and inspires us to
love daily. I have a framed print in my bathroom which
says, "Enjoy the little things in life...For one day you will
look back and realize they were the big things." This,
too, is an important reminder to remember that life's little
moments count just as much as the big ones, and
sometimes even more so. These serve to remind me that
everything matters, and each moment matters. Love is a
gift which recognizes this and lives by it consistently and
purposefully.
Love is a gift given by grace, that is, unmerited favor And
when grace shows us love it also gives us Jesus.

This is the kind of love we see in the face of Jesus.

Love is not complete without Jesus. And that is what my next book will be about. His love the way he loves loved and loves, loved us and the way he loves through us, forgiveness, reconciling love, and many other dimensions of this wondrous love he is given us. That is what my next book will discuss.

CONCLUSION

The gift I hope you have received most of all in reading this book is The Gift of Love – How to recognize it, receive it, and give it. Now you have a clearer knowledge of the Attributes of Love. You have a reference for what love is and what love is not. And as you apply this understanding, your relationships and life will be fuller, more satisfying, and abundant with love.

Where you find love, you will also find peace, patience, goodness, gentleness, self-control, and perseverance. If you have everything in the world but do not have love, you have nothing. Always choose love and pursue it.

"The greatest happiness of life is the conviction that we are loved; loved for ourselves, or rather, loved in spite of ourselves." Victor Hugo

"There is only one happiness in this life: to love and be loved." George Sand

Discovering what I have about love has helped me see these areas in my own life where I have loved well and not loved as well. It has helped me personally to understand why some relationships have worked out well while others have not. And it has improved the quality of my relationships with all kinds of people in my life, from romantic interests, to family, to friends and acquaintances. I hope it helps you as well.

Love has a standard, and its attributes are consistent.

When we learn how to live by love and filter our relationships through it, assessing them, and seeing them for what they are rather than what we wish them to be, it makes all the difference in helping us carve a beautiful, solid path for our lives, a steady road on which we can journey hand and hand with others embracing The Gift. We can also learn more clearly who rejects The Gift. And we know what we can ask of God in prayer to move their hearts toward The Gift.

REFERENCES

Strong's Concordance – Generally known as *Strong's Concordance*, this Bible reference is the leading source on the meaning of Hebrew and Greek words used in the Bible. Its full title is *The Exhaustive Concordance of the Bible*, a compendium under the direction of James Strong.

NET Bible – The NET Bible is the New English Translation of 2005. It is an English online translation of the Bible with extensive translator's notes. It is an online translation prized for its accuracy. It is online, free, and easily available to anyone in the world who has access to the Internet.

Scriptures About Love

If I speak in the tongues of men and of angels, but I do not have love, I am a noisy gong or a clanging cymbal. And if I have prophecy, and know all mysteries and all knowledge, and if I have all faith so that I can remove mountains, but do not have love, I am nothing. If I give away everything I own, and if I give over my body in order to boast, but do not have love, I receive no benefit.

Love is patient, love is kind, it is not envious. Love does not brag, it is not puffed up. It is not rude, it is not self-serving, it is not easily angered or resentful. It is not glad about injustice, but rejoices in the truth. It bears all things, believes all things, hopes all things, endures all things.

Love never ends. But if there are prophecies, they will be set aside; if there are tongues, they will cease; if there is knowledge, it will be set aside. For we know in part, and we prophesy in part, but when what is perfect comes, the partial will be set aside. When I was a child, I talked like a child, I thought like a child, I reasoned like a child. But when I became an adult, I set aside childish ways. For now we see in a mirror indirectly, but then we will see face to face. Now I know in part, but then I will know fully, just as I have been fully known. And now these three remain: faith, hope, and love. But the greatest of these is love.

From 1 Corinthians 13 - *Net Bible*

I have loved you with an everlasting love; I have drawn you with unfailing love.

Jeremiah 31:3

"Teacher, which commandment in the law is the greatest?" Jesus said to him, *"Love the Lord your God with all your heart, with*

all your soul, and with all your mind.' This is the
first and greatest commandment. The second is like it*:
'Love your neighbor as yourself.'* All the law and the
prophets depend on these two commandments."

Matthew 22:36-40

And I pray that you, being rooted and established in love,
may have power, together with all the Lord's holy
people, to grasp how wide and long and high and deep is
the love of Christ, and to know this love that surpasses
knowledge—that you may be filled to the measure of all
the fullness of God.

Ephesians 3:17-19

Whoever does not love does not know God, because
God is love.

1 John 4:8

We love because he first loved us.

1 John 4:19

The Love Test

Is it love?

Take the Love Test to find out.

Check all that apply:

____Patience
____Kindness
____Not envious
____Not boastful
____Not arrogant
____Not unbecoming
____Not self-absorbed
____Not easily angered, exasperated or irritated
____Does not keep score
____Does not engage in destructive thinking, feeling or actions.
____Does not find joy in injustice
____Rejoices in the truth
____Supports and protects
____Believes continuously
____Hopes continuously
____Does not leave
____Is determined to be here to stay.

About The Author

Amanda J. Seymour, Th.M. is an inspirational author, speaker, and motivational consultant who helps people live into what matters most in their lives. She holds a Th.M. from Dallas Theological Seminary and a B.A. in International Studies from Trinity University. Amanda is a recipient of the William N. Garrison Lifestyle Evangelism Award.

She is the founder and director of Deeper Love, an organization which helps people grow in deeper love and fulfillment in every area of their lives. To find out more or reserve Amanda for a speaking engagement or consulting, visit **www.AmandaJSeymour.com.**

Deeper Love

Deeper Love is devoted to bringing deeper love into people's lives in every area. We help people to grow in love and fulfillment in their relationships, families, and communities. Find out more at **www.DeeperLove.net.**

Questions? Comments? Inquiries?

Amanda would love to hear from you!

If you would like to be on our mailing list, to receive an update on upcoming books, or to book Amanda for speaking engagements, conferences, retreats, or consulting, please send an email to amandamail33@gmail.com.

www.ingramcontent.com/pod-product-compliance
Lightning Source LLC
Chambersburg PA
CBHW062024040426
42447CB00010B/2121

* 9 7 8 0 6 9 2 4 1 1 7 0 4 *